TEENAGE MUTANT NINJA TURTLES

VOL. 6 · CITY FALL, PART 1

Story by Kevin Eastman, Bobby Curnow, and Tom Waltz • Script by Tom Waltz

Art by Kevin Eastman and Mateus Santolouco

Special thanks to Joan Hilty, Linda Lee, and Kat van Dam for their invaluable assistance.

nickelodeon™

IDW founded by Ted Adams, Alex Garner, Kris Oprisko, and Robbie Robbins

ISBN: 978-1-61377-783-1

16 15 14 13 1 2 3 4

Originally published as TEENAGE MUTANT NINJA TURTLES issues #21–24.

Additional Art by Dan Duncan, Ross Campbell, Andy Kuhn, Ben Bates, and Mike Henderson

Colors by Ronda Pattison • Letters by Shawn Lee and Tom B. Long

Series Edits by Bobby Curnow

Collection Edits by Justin Eisinger & Alonzo Simon

Collection Design by Chris Mowry • Cover by Mateus Santolouco

Based on characters created by Peter Laird and Kevin Eastman

NEW YORK CITY.
CHAPTER 1
ALL RIGHT, GUYS—TRAINING'S DONE FOR THE NIGHT. DINNER TIME.
MAN, IS IT JUST ME, OR DO THINGS SEEM, I DUNNO... MORE TENSE THAN NORMAL IN THE CITY?
IT'S NOT JUST YOU, DONNIE—I'VE NOTICED IT, TOO. SEEMS LIKE THERE'S BEEN A LOT LESS PETTY CRIME LATELY BUT A LOT MORE VIOLENT STUFF.
ME AND CASEY WERE JUST TALKIN' 'BOUT THE SAME THING THE OTHER DAY. WHOLE DAMN CITY SEEMS TWITCHY FOR SOME REASON.
UH... GUYS...

GAH!
HYAH!
GUYS, DEFEND YOURSELVES!

WHO THE—?

AHH, LOOK... MUTANT TADPOLES. YOU FANCY YOURSELVES NINJA, PERHAPS?
SHALL WE FIND OUT WHAT SKILLS YOU HAVE, LITTLE TADPOLES, HM?
TOO SLOW.
AND NOT TOO SHARP.
THIS MOVE MAY SURPRISE YOU.
MUCH LIKE THIS ONE.
MIGHT I BORROW THIS FOR A MOMENT?
TOO KIND!
KRAK
JUST A MINOR ADJUSTMENT TO SUIT MY NEEDS.

HAVE YOU TOADS EVER HEARD OF THE FILIPINO ART OF KALI, HM?
IT'S AN EXTRAORDINARILY EFFECTIVE FIGHTING FORM USING SHORT STICKS—MUCH LIKE THESE. PERFECT FOR MULTIPLE ATTACKERS.
SHALL I DEMONSTRATE? AFTER ALL...
...SEEING IS BELIEVING!
YOU MAY HAVE SWORDS...
...AND SAI...
...NUNCHAKU, EVEN.
BUT SKILLS?
SADLY, NO.
BANG! BANG! YOU TADPOLES ARE DEAD.
SUCH DREADFUL STUDENTS—I PITY THE FAILED TEACHER WHO TRAINED YOU SO POORLY.

AND THAT WOULD BE THE OLD, DECREPIT RAT...
...HIDING IN THAT OLD, DECREPIT CHURCH, HM?
ADIEU!
WHO...
...THE HELL...
...WAS...
...THAT?
HE KNOWS ABOUT FATHER.
AND THE CHURCH!
OH... MAN.
LET'S MOVE!

NO MORE MESSING AROUND, GUYS—WE STOP THIS CLOWN, WHATEVER IT TAKES!
I CAN'T BELIEVE HE BROKE MY STAFF.
THAT'S NOTHIN' COMPARED TO THE WAY I'M GONNA BREAK HIS FACE AFTER I SLAP THAT STUPID MASK OFFA IT!

MAN, HE'S FAST!
THIS GUY FOOT, OR WHAT?
THE WAY HE WAS FIGHTING, HE'S GOTTA BE!
WHICH WAY'D HE GO?
NINTH STREET MARKET
DOWN HERE!
I'LL GIVE YOU THREE GUESSES.
A NOTE? SERIOUSLY?
HANG TIGHT, GUYS. THIS IS A SETUP.
OH YEAH?
BRING IT!
RAPH! WAIT!
AH, THE IMPETUOUS STUDENTS...
...HERE FOR YOUR FRENCH LESSONS, HM?
ALLEZ OUP!
HE'S MOVING JUST LIKE THOSE FRENCH SAVATE GUYS!
FRENCH? I THOUGHT HE WAS FILIPINO.
YOU RECOGNIZE MY STYLE?
NOT COMPLETELY BRAINLESS, IT APPEARS.
KLOP
YET STUPID NONETHELESS.

THE ART OF FINE CUISINE IS BUT ONE OF MANY THINGS THE FRENCH EXCEL AT.
TAKE THE ARTS OF SAVATE AND PARKOUR, FOR EXAMPLE.
TODAY'S LESSON INCLUDES...
...CHASSE!
FREE RUNNING!
REVERS!
REDISTRIBUTION!
YAH!
WHOULF!
FOUETTE!
GNF!
AND, FINALLY, LIKE ANY TRUE TRACEUR...
...TRACE!
...LEAVE...
...NO...

CRIPES! HE'S GONE AGAIN! THIS GUY IS QUICK.
YEAH, QUICK TO RUN AWAY LIKE A SCARED LITTLE CHICKEN.
YOU MEAN THE SCARED LITTLE CHICKEN THAT JUST KICKED THE CRAP OUT OF US?
SHUT UP, MIKEY.
ALL OF YOU SHUT UP AND LISTEN. WE NEED TO REGROUP... FOCUS.
HE HAD THE SURPRISE, BUT THAT'S OVER NOW—AND WE'VE GOT NUMBERS AND FATHER'S TRAINING ON OUR SIDE.
NOW HE'S GONNA HAVE TO FACE US ON OUR HOME TURF.
CAREFUL, GUYS... THIS DUDE'S SNEAKY...
...HE COULD BE ANYWHERE.
BOO!
AAAH!

HA HA HA HA!

SONUVA—!
AH, THE WILLFUL LEADER...

...PREDICTABLE AS EVER.
UNLIKE ME!
GRF!

YES, DIFFERENT STYLE...
HE'S CHANGING STYLES AGAIN!

...SAME RESULTS!
HRK!

WING CHUN, FOR THE MOST PART, IS MADE UP OF PRECISE BLOCKS AND COUNTERING HAND STRIKES.

NOT TO MENTION...

AHH!
...NERVE STRIKES!

WHEN THESE ELEMENTS ARE COMBINED...

...IT IS PERFECT FOR DEFEATING FOUR CLUMSY OPPONENTS...

...WHO ARE FLAILING USELESSLY...

...IN WAIST-DEEP WATER.

WHILE I REMAIN LIKE A STALK OF BAMBOO.

FIRM BUT FLEXIBLE.
ROOTED BUT YIELDING.

I'LL BAMBOO YOU, YA STINKIN' FOOT JER—
I THINK...
...NOT!
GAK!

IT MATTERS NOT HOW YOU ATTACK—I WILL SIMPLY GLIDE THROUGH YOU LIKE THE WIND...
...CHOOSING THE MOMENT WHEN I STRIKE.
IT SEEMS I WAS MISTAKEN, HM? YOU FOUR DO POSSESS GREAT SKILL.
YOU HAVE MASTERED THE ART OF FAILING.
I AM NEITHER FOOT NOR SAVATE. I LURK IN THE SHADOWS, THE UNKNOWN FOE. YOU DO NOT KNOW ME YET... BUT YOU WILL.

AND SO, I HAVE DEFEATED THE STUDENTS. NOW IT IS MY RIGHT TO FACE THE SENSEI IN HIS DOJO. FAREWELL!
RAAGH!
BASTARD'S GONNA PAY!

JUST COOL IT AND HURRY, GUYS!
THE CHURCH IS ONLY A FEW BLOCKS AWAY!

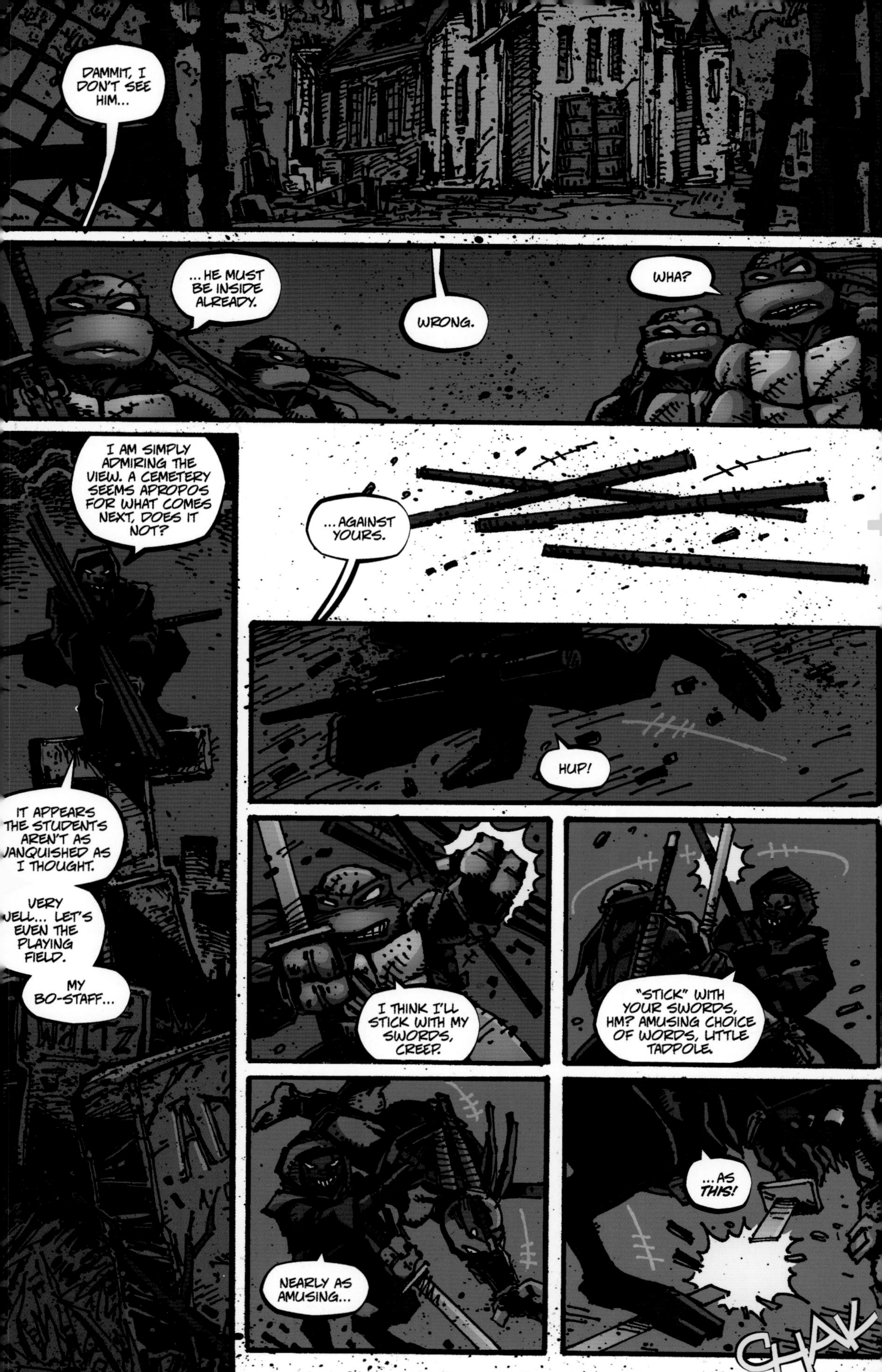

DAMMIT, I DON'T SEE HIM...
...HE MUST BE INSIDE ALREADY.
WRONG.
WHA?
I AM SIMPLY ADMIRING THE VIEW. A CEMETERY SEEMS APROPOS FOR WHAT COMES NEXT, DOES IT NOT?
IT APPEARS THE STUDENTS AREN'T AS VANQUISHED AS I THOUGHT.
VERY WELL... LET'S EVEN THE PLAYING FIELD.
MY BO-STAFF...
...AGAINST YOURS.
HUP!
I THINK I'LL STICK WITH MY SWORDS, CREEP.
"STICK" WITH YOUR SWORDS, HM? AMUSING CHOICE OF WORDS, LITTLE TADPOLE.
NEARLY AS AMUSING...
...AS THIS!
CHAK

I, FOR ONE, CHOOSE TO STICK WITH MY STICK.
SHALL WE BEGIN?
YOU'RE GOING DOWN!
EVENTUALLY. BUT, FIRST...
...UP.
OVER.
UNDER.
CENTER.
THROUGH.
BETWEEN.
ABOVE.
BEHIND.
AND, FINALLY, YES...
...DOWN.
WELL, THAT WAS ENJOYABLE, BUT TIME FLIES, AS THE SAYING GOES.
AND I DON'T WANT TO BE LATE FOR MY DATE WITH YOUR TEACHER.
WHAM

HOLD UP!
YEAH. WE AIN'T DONE WITH YOU YET, CREEPY.
SO, YOU WOULD DANCE WITH ME AGAIN, LITTLE TADPOLES?
WELL, I SUPPOSE FOOLISHNESS WOULD NOT EXIST WITHOUT PERSISTENCE, WOULD IT?
FAR BE IT FROM ME TO REFUSE.

HRK!

PLEASE UNDERSTAND, HOWEVER...

FWAK

...THAT WHEN IT COMES TO DANCING...

...I ALWAYS PREFER TO TAKE THE LEAD.

SO, ONLY ONE DANCE PARTNER REMAINS, HM?
I'M NOT YOUR PARTNER.
NO, YOU ARE NOT. THAT WOULD IMPLY YOU ARE MY EQUAL.

I'M GETTING SICK AND TIRED OF ALL YOUR BRAGGING, MAN. YOU CAUGHT US BY SURPRISE AND MADE US PAY FOR IT—I'LL GIVE YOU THAT MUCH.
BUT YOU'RE IN OUR HOUSE NOW—OUR DOJO—AND WE WON'T LET YOU DISRESPECT OUR HOME... OR OUR MASTER. **EVER.**
WE SHALL SEE.
UFF!
YES, WE WILL!
MY FATHER GAVE ME THE BO-STAFF YOU BROKE!
AND WHEN HE GAVE IT TO ME, HE TOLD ME SOMETHING I'LL NEVER FORGET.
ERK!
HE SAID, "THIS STAFF IS NO BETTER OR WORSE THAN ANY OTHER, MY SON..."
"...WHAT MATTERS MOST IS THE HONOR AND SKILLS OF HE WHO WIELDS IT."
IT'S WHAT HE TOLD US ALL.

SO, YOU HAVE SOME COURAGE IN YOU AFTER ALL. PITY YOU'VE FOUND IT TOO LATE.
I AM THROUGH TOYING WITH THE FOUR OF YOU--OUR GAME ENDS NOW.
HATE TO DISAPPOINT YOU AND ALL, BUT NOTHIN' ENDS TILL WE SAY IT DOES!
YEAH, DUDE! WE'RE JUST GETTING' WARMED UP!
YOUR BRAGGADOCIO IS PRECIOUS. BUT I MUST DISAPPOINT YOU.
THE TIME HAS COME FOR ME TO CALL ON YOUR MASTER.

THEN UNDERSTAND THIS—THE ONLY WAY TO OUR MASTER IS *OVER OUR DEAD BODIES.*

THEN I CAN ONLY RESPOND THAT I AM HONORED...
...MY SONS.

FATHER?!
PLEASE, FORGIVE ME THIS SHOCK—I REALIZE THIS MUST BE DIFFICULT FOR YOU, JUST AS IT IS DIFFICULT FOR A FATHER TO BE SO HARD ON HIS SONS, EVEN WHEN HE KNOWS HE MUST.

TRUE BALANCE COMES, MY SONS, NOT ONLY FROM LEARNING, BUT FROM UN-LEARNING, AS WELL.

YOU HAVE EACH MASTERED THE FIGHTING STYLES I HAVE TAUGHT YOU. BUT AS OUR MANY BATTLES HAVE SURELY SHOWN US, OUR ENEMIES DO NOT ALWAYS BEHAVE IN A PREDICTABLE WAY... AND NEITHER SHOULD WE.
I, LIKE YOU, SENSE AN ILL WIND BLOWING THROUGH THIS CITY. ONE THAT WE SHOULD NOT—*MUST* NOT—IGNORE IF WE ARE TO SURVIVE.
SO, OPEN YOUR HEARTS AND MINDS NOW, MY SONS—YOUR REAL TRAINING BEGINS TONIGHT. WE MUST PREPARE OURSELVES. AS EVER...

"... WE CANNOT BE CERTAIN WHO... OR WHAT... AWAITS IN THE SHADOWS."

JAPAN.

YOU ARE CERTAIN, DOCTOR MILLER, THAT THIS IS THE PLACE?

YES, IT HAS TO BE...

I AM DOUBTFUL, GRANDFATHER. AFTER ALL THIS TIME... THESE MANY YEARS... HOW COULD SOMETHING LIKE THIS GO UNDISCOV—
MASTER SHREDDER...

...WE HAVE FOUND SOMETHING!

THEN WHY DO YOU WASTE TIME, FOOL? BRING IT OUT!

YES, MASTER!

WELL, DOCTOR MILLER, IT APPEARS YOU HAVE PROVEN YOUR WORTH.
UTTERLY... FASCINATING.
INDEED.
WELCOME, AT LAST, TO THE NEW AGE...

...KITSUNE.

CHAPTER 2
NEW YORK CITY.
<OUR RIVALS, THE SAVATE, HAVE RECENTLY FOUND A NEW LEADER...> *
* SEE TMNT ANNUAL #1 – B.C.

<"...A WARRIOR NAMED VICTOR, WHO OPPOSES MY AUTHORITY.>
<"RECENT SAVATE ADVANCEMENTS HAVE... EMBOLDENED OTHER UNDERWORLD ELEMENTS TO FOLLOW SUIT.">

<"THESE NEW ALLIES HAVE SUCCESSFULLY RAIDED OUR MATERIEL SHIPMENTS.>
<"WE CONTINUE TO MEET VICTOR'S CHALLENGES AT EVERY TURN...>
<"...BUT HE REMAINS STUBBORN.">

<MY PATIENCE FOR SUCH MATTERS IS AT AN END.>
<WHAT, THEN, DO YOU PROPOSE, OROKU SAKI?>
<WHAT WE HAVE ALWAYS DONE, KITSUNE...>

CITY FALL
PART ONE
<...EMBRACE OUR DESTINY.>

skara brae
CAN WE GO OR WHAT, CASEY?

I DON'T KNOW 'BOUT YOU, MAN, BUT I'M GETTIN' BORED—

"—OF STARIN' AT YOUR OLD MAN DRINKIN' THE PLACE DRY."

SORRY, RAPH. IT'S JUST... MAN, DON'T HE LOOK BAD TO YOU? I MEAN, MORE THAN NORMAL?
YEAH, WELL...

...YOU'D THINK A BEATDOWN FROM MASTER SPLINTER WOULDA SOBERED HIS BUTT UP. GUESS SOME CHUMPS NEVER LEARN, HUH?
YEAH... MAYBE.

skara brae
C'MON, LET'S GO— I'VE SEEN ENOUGH.
FINALLY!
DUDE, AFTER ALL THE NASTY CRAP THAT GUY DID TO YOU, I GOT NO CLUE WHY YOU WASTE TIME CHECKIN' IN ON HIM.

I KNOW IT DON'T MAKE SENSE, BUT I MADE A PROMISE TO MY MOM, SO I'M DOIN' IT FOR HER.
MOSTLY.
WELL, I CAME OUT TO KICK SOME BAD-GUY BUTT, NOT WATCH YOU KICK YOUR OWN, OKAY? SO WHY DON'T—
FOOT! ATTACK!
DAMN! WHERE THE HELL'D THESE GUYS COME FROM?!
YOU'RE ASKIN' ME?!
DON'T YOU GOT NINJA SUPER-SENSE OR SOMETHIN'?
YEAH, I LEARNED THAT RIGHT AFTER I FIGURED OUT HOW TO SHOOT LASERS FROM MY EYES. SHEESH!
THERE'S A TON OF THESE G—
KRAK
HRK!
CASEY!

STINKIN'... DIRTY... FOOT SCUM...

I'M GONNA KICK ALL YOUR—

BRING DOWN THE MUTANT!

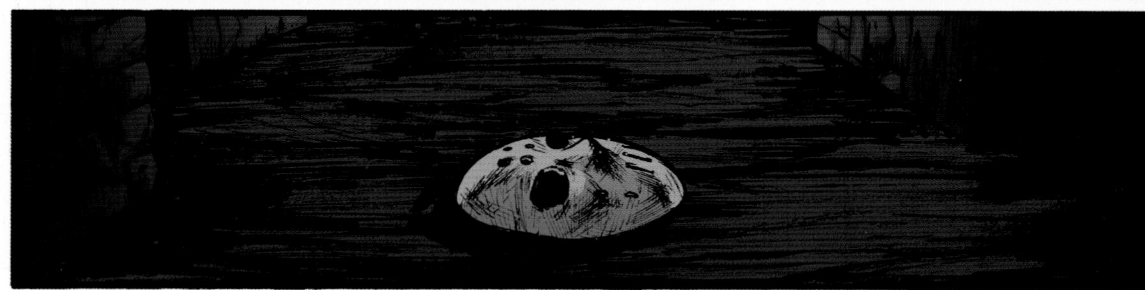

MRRMFF! ERFMF!
SO, MUTANT...

...WE MEET AGAIN.
THE DISCOMFORT YOU ARE EXPERIENCING IS ONLY TEMPORARY.

IT WILL END SOON...WHEN YOU PERISH.

DRIVER! TAKE US TO THE DOCKS!

CSHKK

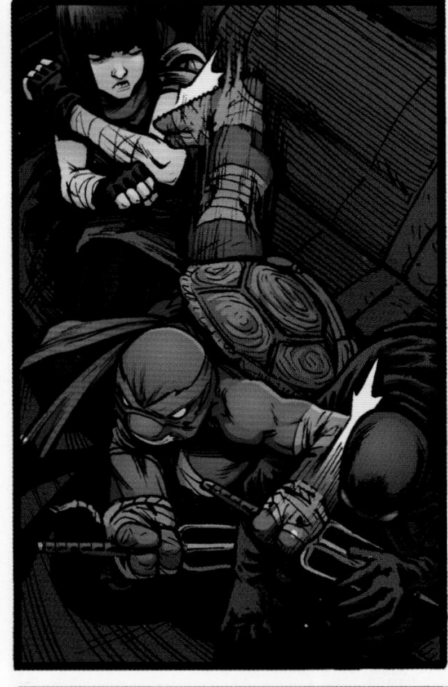

WHAM

SPLASH

THE MUTANT IS GONE.
YES...

"...ALL IS GOING TO PLAN."

HYAH!

WHOA!

KLAK

I DIDN'T EVEN SEE THAT COMING, MASTER SPLINTER.

THAT IS BECAUSE, BY BRINGING THE *SHINAI* TO MY LEFT SHOULDER IN A *KATSUGI*—JUST SO—I DREW YOUR ATTENTION TO MY SURPRISE MOTION...

...AND YOU OPENED YOURSELF TO MY ATTACK AS A RESULT.

THE FULL TECHNIQUE IS CALLED *KATSUGI MEN*—AN EXCELLENT MANEUVER IF PRACTICED SPARINGLY. IF OVERUSED, AN EXPERIENCED OPPONENT WILL LOOK TO COUNTER *KATSUGI* WITH A *DEBANA WAZA.*

GOOD TO KNOW.

AND I'VE EVEN GOT SENSORS SET UP IN THE CHURCH... HERE AND HERE.
WOW! YOU'VE BEEN BUSY, DONNIE.
WELL, IF SLASH TAUGHT US ANYTHING, IT'S THAT YOU CAN'T BE TOO CAREFUL.

AND DON'T FORGET HOB AND THOSE STUPID MOUSERS.
100-PAGE SPECTACULAR 2012
Alter
NO, MIKEY—NOBODY'S FORGOTTEN THEM.

AND NOW THAT SECURITY'S SET, WE CAN GET TO TESTING THIS OOZE YOU TOOK FROM STOCKGEN AND WORKING ON THE TECHNODROME PROBLEM.

BEEP
BEEP
BEEP
WHAT IN THE WORLD?

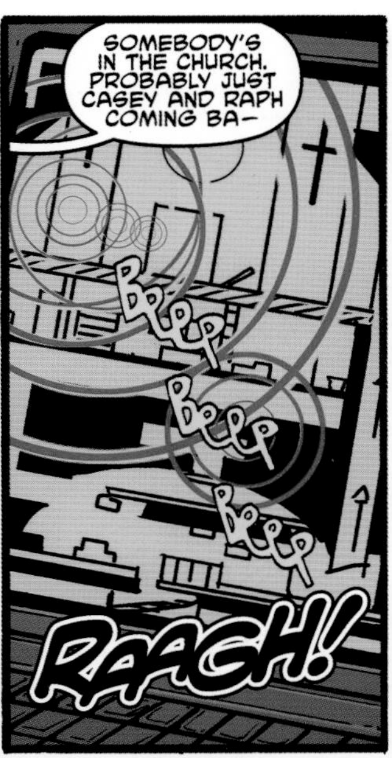

SOMEBODY'S IN THE CHURCH. PROBABLY JUST CASEY AND RAPH COMING BA–
BEEP
BEEP
BEEP
RAAGH!

UM, THAT DIDN'T SOUND LIKE CASEY OR RAPH.
OH, MAN! I THINK IT'S SLASH! IT'S SLASH, ISN'T IT?!
REMAIN CALM, MICHELANGELO.

WHAT'S EVERYONE JUST STANDIN' AROUND FOR? WE GOTTA GET GOIN'—THEY GOT CASEY!

RAPHAEL—YOU MUST GATHER YOURSELF. WHAT HAP–
WE DON'T GOT TIME! THEY TOOK CASEY AND WE GOTTA GO GET HIM BACK!

SLOW DOWN, RAPH—WHO TOOK CASEY?
KARAI AND THOSE FOOT FREAKS—BUNCH OF 'EM JUMPED US. I GOT AWAY BUT CASEY GOT KNOCKED COLD AND I THINK THEY WERE TAKIN' HIM TO THE DOCKS.
I'M TELLIN' YA, WE GOTTA GET MOVIN'!
OH NO.

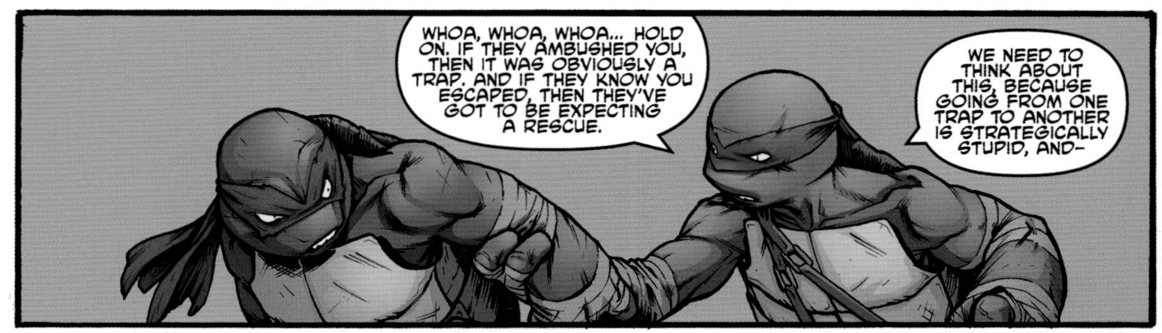
WHOA, WHOA, WHOA... HOLD ON. IF THEY AMBUSHED YOU, THEN IT WAS OBVIOUSLY A TRAP. AND IF THEY KNOW YOU ESCAPED, THEN THEY'VE GOT TO BE EXPECTING A RESCUE.
WE NEED TO THINK ABOUT THIS, BECAUSE GOING FROM ONE TRAP TO ANOTHER IS STRATEGICALLY STUPID, AND–

DAMMIT, LEO, WE GOT NO TIME FOR NINJA TACTICAL CRAP—THIS IS MY BEST FRIEND WE'RE TALKIN' ABOUT... OUR *FAMILY*, MAN. HE NEEDS US *NOW!*
YEAH, AND RUSHING INTO TROUBLE'S REALLY WORKED OUT FOR YOU TWO IN THE PAST, RIGHT?
YOU STINKIN'–
STOP!

STAND APART, MY SONS.
WE ACHIEVE NOTHING IF WE QUARREL AMONGST OURSELVES.

YOU ARE BOTH CORRECT. CASEY JONES IS PART OF OUR FAMILY AND WE MUST SAVE HIM, BUT IT WOULD BE FOOLHARDY TO DO SO IN RECKLESS FASHION.
WE MUST BE QUICK... BUT WE MUST ALSO BE CAUTIOUS.

REST ASSURED, RAPHAEL, WE WILL DO EVERYTHING IN OUR POWER...

"...TO RESCUE YOUR FRIEND."
IS ALL IN ORDER?
YES...

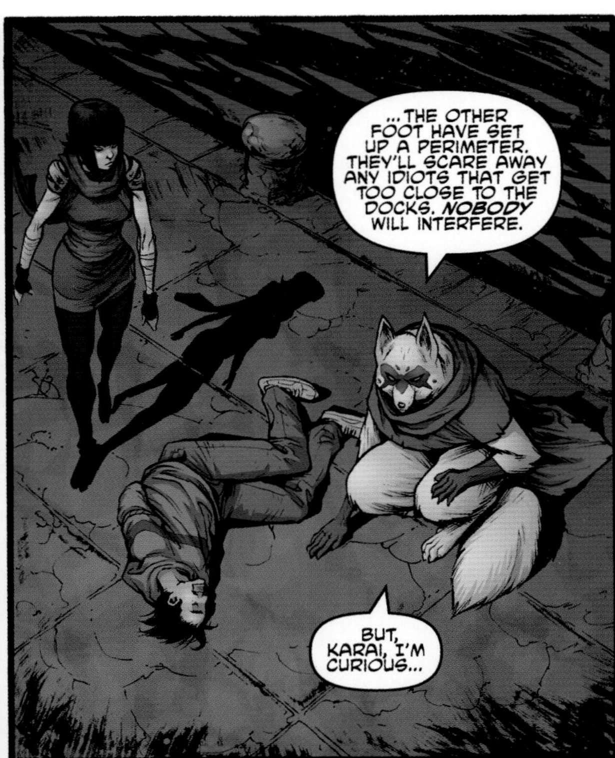

...THE OTHER FOOT HAVE SET UP A PERIMETER. THEY'LL SCARE AWAY ANY IDIOTS THAT GET TOO CLOSE TO THE DOCKS. *NOBODY* WILL INTERFERE.
BUT, KARAI, I'M CURIOUS...

...WHAT MAKES YOU SO *SURE* THEY'LL COME FOR THEIR FRIEND?

I KNOW THEY WILL COME, ALOPEX, BECAUSE THEY ARE NINJA. A *CLAN*.

FOOLISHLY LOYAL UNTO DEATH.

OKAY, GUYS, WE'RE HERE.

MISS O'NEIL, UNTIL WE UNDERSTAND EXACTLY *WHAT* IT IS WE ARE FACING, I MUST ASK THAT YOU STAY BEHIND.
NO PROBLEM, MASTER SPLINTER.

AND LISTEN, FOOT OR NO FOOT, THIS AIN'T THE BEST 'HOOD IN TOWN. LOCK THIS THING UP *TIGHT* AND KEEP THE MOTOR RUNNIN' JUST IN CASE WE GOTTA *BOOGIE* THE HELL OUTTA HERE, OKAY?
OKAY, RAPH. JUST STAY SAFE, ALL RIGHT?
AND, *PLEASE*... GET CASEY BACK.
DON'T WORRY...

...I *WILL*.

'NIGHT, DAD. SEE YOU LA—

WHAT THE HELL?

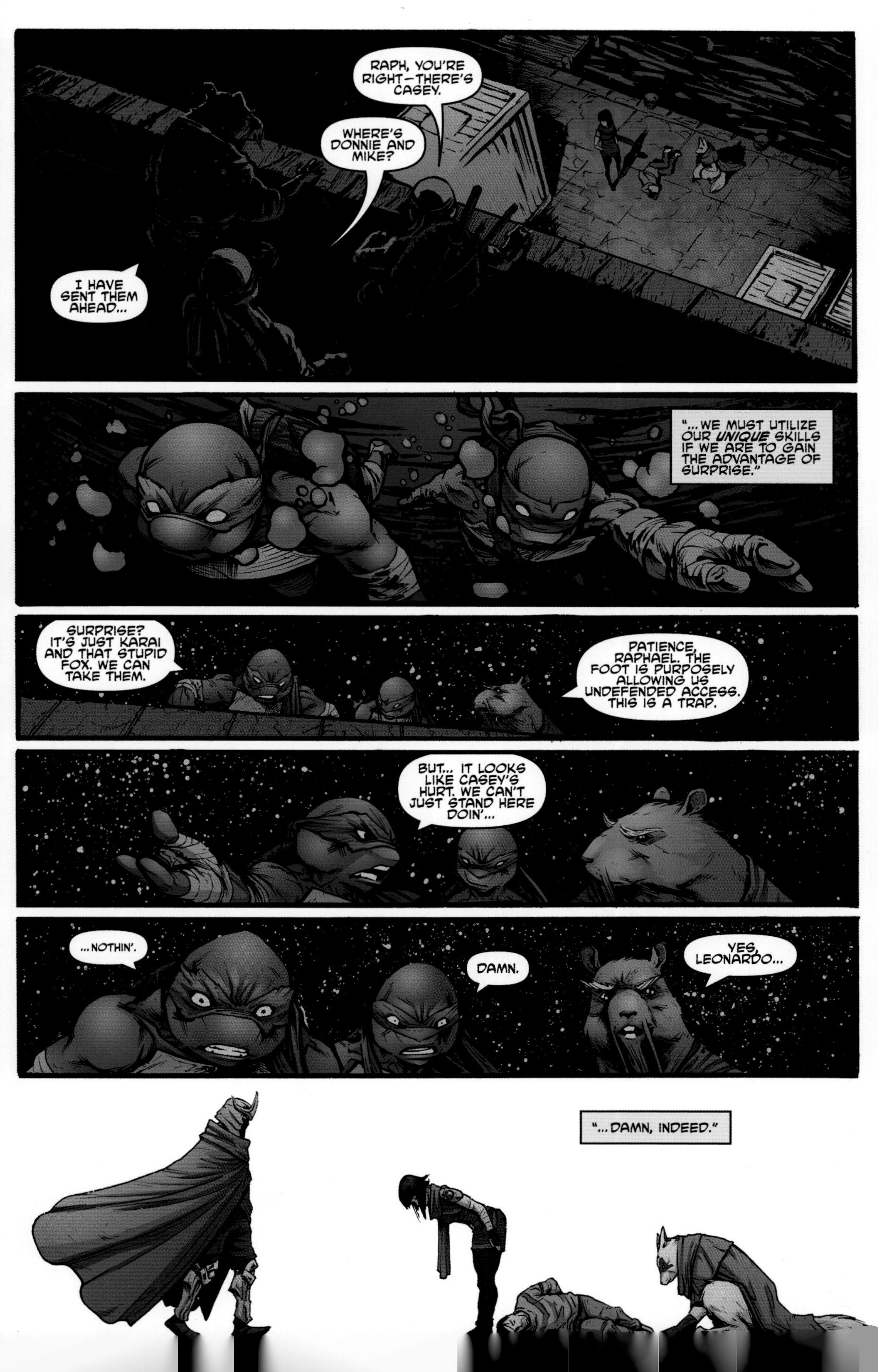
RAPH, YOU'RE RIGHT—THERE'S CASEY.
WHERE'S DONNIE AND MIKE?
I HAVE SENT THEM AHEAD...
"...WE MUST UTILIZE OUR *UNIQUE* SKILLS IF WE ARE TO GAIN THE ADVANTAGE OF SURPRISE."
SURPRISE? IT'S JUST KARAI AND THAT STUPID FOX. WE CAN TAKE THEM.
PATIENCE, RAPHAEL. THE FOOT IS PURPOSELY ALLOWING US UNDEFENDED ACCESS. THIS IS A TRAP.
BUT... IT LOOKS LIKE CASEY'S HURT. WE CAN'T JUST STAND HERE DOIN'...
...NOTHIN'.
DAMN.
YES, LEONARDO...
"...DAMN, INDEED."

KNOCK
KNOCK
HOLY CRAP!

OH, MY GOD... YOU ABOUT GAVE ME A HEART ATTACK, UM...
ANGEL.
YOU'RE THAT COLLEGE CHICK WHO HANGS WITH CASEY, AIN'T YOU? WHAT THE HELL YOU DOIN' HERE?

THE... THE FOOT KIDNAPPED CASEY, SO THE GUYS—SPLINTER AND THE TURTLES—AND I CAME DOWN HERE TO GET HIM BACK.
KIDNAPPED? WHEN?
EARLIER TONIGHT. HE MIGHT BE HURT...

...OR WORSE.

DAMN.

WHAT'S YOUR NAME?
APRIL.
WHERE WERE THE OTHERS GOIN', APRIL?
THE DOCKS. RAPH HEARD KARAI SAY THAT'S WHERE THEY WERE TAKING CASEY.

OKAY. I GOTTA GO HELP 'EM. CASEY'S THE ONLY REASON I AIN'T IN JAIL OR DEAD RIGHT NOW.
BY YOURSELF?
NO TIME TO GET THE OTHER DRAGONS. YOU HANG TIGHT.
YEAH, YEAH... AND LOCK MY DOORS. I KNOW, I KNOW...

THEY ARE HERE, GRANDFATHER.
YES, KARAI.
I KNOW YOU ARE OUT THERE, HAMATO YOSHI! WHY DO YOU DELAY COMING TO THE AID OF YOUR FALLEN COMRADE?!
WHY DO YOU HIDE?!
MASTER, DO YOU WANT ME TO GO AFTER THEM? CHASE THEM OUT?
NO, ALOPEX, THERE IS NO NEED TO PURSUE THEM.
I WILL SHOW YOU HOW TO DRAW VERMIN TO A TRAP.
MMFM... FMMF... MMF...?
YOSHI, YOUR UNDIVIDED ATTENTION IS REQUIRED! AS YOU CAN SEE...
MRFMF... URFF... MMFF!

SCHLIP
...YOUR COMRADE IS NOW *SEVERELY WOUNDED!*

MY SON, WAIT!
NO!
FOOT! ATTACK!
GRRAAGH!
WITH ME, ALOPEX. AS WE PLANNED--AVOID THE BATTLE AND DO NOT LOSE SIGHT OF THE TARGET.
THAT BASTARD STABBED HIM!
RAPHAEL, CALM YOURSELF! FOCUS!
LISTEN TO FATHER, RAPH!
I'M GONNA KILL HIM!

ALL HELL'S BREAKING LOOSE!
C'MON, MIKEY—WE GOTTA GET CASEY!
COMIN'!

AH, AN AMPHIBIOUS ASSAULT. CLEVER STRATEGY... ALBEIT A PREDICTABLE ONE.
WE'RE *REPTILES*, YOU DOOFUS!
THAT'S NOT WHAT HE MEANT, MIKEY.

OH, NO...

"...CASEY."

LEONARDO, ASSIST YOUR OTHER BROTHERS—I WILL STAY WITH RAPHAEL!
YES, SENSEI!
RAPHAEL!
I'M GONNA RIP YOU APART!

OUR TARGET IS IN THE OPEN, ALOPEX—YOU KNOW WHAT TO DO.
YES. KEEP THE PREY SEPARATED FROM THE HERD.
GRRARGH!
WHUMP
WHAT THE—UFF!
GUYS—CASEY'S HURT BAD! WE GOTTA GET HIM OUTTA HERE!
I—GRF!—NEED HELP!
DON! MIKE! HELP ANGEL!
C'MON, MIKEY! FORGET THIS GUY!
SEE YOU 'ROUND, PINHEAD!
YES...
...YOU WILL.

ANGEL! WHERE'D YOU COME FROM?
LATER! LET'S GO!
LEO, COME ON!
WORKING ON IT!
FATHER! WE HAVE CASEY!

I'M OUTTA HERE!

FWP
YAH!

WHUMP

IT IS DONE, MASTER.
YES, KARAI. I SEE.

EXCELLENT.

OH, MAN... CASEY.
HIS WOUND IS DEEP. WE MUST GET HIM TO A HOSPITAL IMMEDIATELY.
DUDES, THE FOOT JUST TOTALLY TOOK OFF!

APRIL!
I HEARD ALL THE NOISE AND COULDN'T SIT AROUND WAITING ANYMORE, SO I—
—OH, MY GOD.

C'MON, WE GOTTA HURRY!
FATHER, LEO'S NOT HERE!
LEONARDO? BUT—
OH, MAN...

DAMMIT, WE DON'T HAVE TIME!
SHE'S RIGHT...
...CASEY'S DYING!

CHAPTER 3
WE'RE ALMOST THERE...
...I CALLED AHEAD, SO THEY SHOULD BE READY FOR US.
LET US HOPE THEY ARE, MISS O'NEIL. HE HAS LOST MUCH BLOOD. I FEAR WITHOUT PROPER MEDICAL CARE, HE HAS LITTLE TIME.
OH, GOD... CASEY...
WE ARE NEARLY THERE, MASTER...
...KITSUNE AND HER PRIESTS ARE STANDING BY.
EXCELLENT.

EMERGENCY
SKREEEEE

WHAT HAPPENED?
WHAT THE HELL'S IT LOOK LIKE?! HE WAS STABBED!
I'LL BE JUST A SEC, ANGEL.

COAST'S CLEAR, GUYS.
I'M GONNA HEAD INSIDE, SEE IF I CAN HELP IN ANY WAY.
THANK YOU, MISS O'NEIL—WE MUST GO.
DONATELLO AND MICHELANGELO ARE SEARCHING FOR LEONARDO WITH ORDERS TO MEET US AT THE LAIR IN ONE HOUR.

SKREEEEE

WHAT DO YOU REQUIRE NEXT, GRANDFATHER?
THERE IS NOTHING I NEED FROM YOU, KARAI.

YOU ARE BOTH DISMISSED.

TAKE HIM TO O.R.-3 AND GET HIM PREPPED ASAP! I'LL BE THERE IN FIVE MINUTES!
QUICKLY, YOU FOOLS!

YOUR FRIEND'S IN PRETTY BAD SHAPE, MISS—MIND TELLING ME WHAT HAPPENED?
I ALREADY TOLD THAT OTHER GUY—HE GOT MUGGED AND STABBED.
LET ME GUESS—THE MUGGER HAD A SWORD, RIGHT? WE'VE BEEN GETTING A LOT OF THESE KIND OF "MUGGINGS" LATELY—YOU KNOW, THE SWORD KIND—AND I'M WONDERING WHY THAT IS.

NO ANSWER, HUH?
WELL, WAIT HERE IF YOU WANT. I NEED TO GO SAVE YOUR FRIEND'S LIFE.
WHAT'D HE SAY, ANGEL?

NOTHIN' GOOD.

<YOU UNDERSTAND HOW IMPORTANT THE NEXT PHASE IS, YES, KITSUNE?>
<OF COURSE. I WILL DELIVER THE FAITHFUL AND ADEPT CHUNIN YOU DESIRE, JUST AS I CONQUERED DEATH'S DARK DOMINION TO BRING YOU TO THIS NEW AGE.>*
<OUR ULTIMATE DESTINY IS WITHIN REACH, SAKI, I PROMISE.>
*See TMNT Secret History of the Foot – B.C.

<MY DESTINY, KITSUNE.>
<AH... JUST SO, MY LORD. JUST SO.>
DOES KITSUNE HAVE NEED OF ASSISTANCE, MASTER?

NO, KARAI...

"...WHAT COMES NEXT REQUIRES A SINGULAR MASTERY POSSESSED ONLY BY AN EXTRAORDINARY FEW."

...BUT THIS IS THE ONLY CLUE WE COULD FIND.

HIS... SWORD? THEN THE FOOT—

UH, GUYS... THAT MIGHT NOT BE THE *ONLY* CLUE...

...CHECK IT OUT!

EAST RIVER
MIDNITE! CAN HELP U! HOB*

GREAT. NOW WE HAVE TO WORRY ABOUT *HOB* KNOWING WHERE WE LIVE.

BUT... WHAT IF HE CAN HELP US LIKE IT SAYS?

DON'T BE STUPID, MIKE. THIS IS HOB, REMEMBER? WE DON'T EVEN KNOW IF HE'S TALKIN' 'BOUT LEO.

NO... WE DO NOT. YET, I FIND IT DIFFICULT TO BELIEVE THE TIMING OF THIS NOTE IS MERE COINCIDENCE.

IF THERE IS EVEN THE SLIGHTEST POSSIBILITY OLD HOB HAS INFORMATION THAT HELPS US FIND LEONARDO, THEN WE MUST HEED HIS INVITATION.

IN THE MEANTIME, WE CAN ONLY HOPE...

"...THAT YOUR BROTHER REMAINS UNHARMED, WHEREVER HE MAY BE."
SO, IT IS ONLY YOU AND I NOW.
I AM CALLED KITSUNE.
WHAT I AM IS BEYOND YOUR MORTAL COMPREHENSION. AND YET, DESPITE APPEARANCES, I AM NOTHING YOU NEED FEAR.
I POSE NO THREAT TO YOU. I AM SIMPLY HERE TO GUIDE YOU...
...TO UNCOVER YOUR EYES AND SHOW YOU THE TRUE MENACE THAT LURKS WITHIN THE DARKEST SHADOWS OF YOUR LIFE.
AND REVEAL TO YOU WHERE YOUR ULTIMATE SALVATION LIES!

"AND WHERE BETTER TO START, YOUNG LEONARDO, THAN THE BEGINNING?
"THE BEGINNING OF THE LIES."
I WILL ALWAYS PROTECT YOU FROM HARM.
MY SON, YOU NEED NOT FEAR.
WHERE IS YOUR GRATITUDE?
YOU SAID... SAID YOU WOULD KEEP US SAFE!
HELP!
IT IS ALL RIGHT, LEONARDO!
YOU DISAPPOINT ME, MY PUPIL.
I AM HERE NOW!

YOU WILL ALWAYS BE SAFE WITH ME, IN OUR HOME.

DO YOU SEE? ALL IS WELL. FATHER HAS EVEN BROUGHT A GIFT FOR YOU.

YOU... YOU SAVED ME.
A TRUE SENSEI KNOWS WHAT IS NEEDED WHEN DANGER APPROACHES— ALWAYS ACTION, NEVER WORDS.

NOW, RUN, CHILD...
...RUN!

WHA... HOW?
OH, NO.
"OH, YES, LEONARDO, DO YOU BEGIN TO SEE? THE BROKEN PROMISES... THE EMPTY WORDS...
"...THE DEEDS OF LOWLY VERMIN."
LEONARDO! THIS WAY-- QUICKLY!
MASTER?!
WH-WHOA!
FOOL. YOU ARE NOT AWARE OF YOUR SURROUNDINGS.
HAVE I TRAINED YOU SO POORLY?
BUT... F-FATHER... GRK... YOU... YOU CALLED TO ME...
I DID NO SUCH THING.

NO! GET AWAY FROM ME!
FASTER, LEONARDO! TO ME!
I'M COMING, SENSEI!
KRSSH
BE STRONG...
...I HAVE YOU.
WAIT—THAT WAS YOU... *YOUR VOICE* I HEARD.
YES. I WAS CALLING YOU AWAY FROM THE WEAKNESS THAT STIFLES YOUR TRUE POTENTIAL. NOW...
...*LEAVE IT BEHIND!*
NO!
AAAAAH AAH

THIS STUFF TASTES LIKE SLUDGE, BUT AT LEAST IT PACKS A PUNCH. SEEMS LIKE WE'VE BEEN HERE FOREVER AND THEY STILL AIN'T TELLIN' US NOTHIN'.
MAYBE NO NEWS IS GOOD NEWS. HE WAS HURT SO BADLY.
UM... ANGEL, THERE'S SOMETHING I WANNA ASK—IF IT'S NOT TOO PERSONAL.
EARLIER TONIGHT, YOU SAID CASEY'S THE ONLY REASON YOU'RE NOT IN JAIL OR DEAD AND... WELL, I'M WONDERING WHAT YOU MEANT.
OH... THAT.
CASEY'S OLD MAN AND MINE USED TO BE TOTAL BADASSES. AND BEST FRIENDS—REAL TIGHT.
ANYWAY, ME AND CASEY WERE BORN 'ROUND THE SAME TIME, AND OUR DADS BOTH TRIED TO GET ON THE RIGHT TRACK. MY DAD STARTED RUNNIN' THE SKARA BRAE AND CASEY'S DAD DID SOME CONSTRUCTION. THEY STAYED CLOSE, SO ME AND CASEY KINDA GREW UP TOGETHER.
BUT THEN CASEY'S MOM GOT SICK AND HIS DAD STARTED BOOZIN' BIG TIME—AND IT GOT WAY WORSE AFTER SHE DIED.
THEN MY MOM... SHE GOT KILLED IN A CAR CRASH AND, WELL... I DIDN'T HANDLE IT SO GOOD—STARTED RUNNIN' WITH THE DRAGONS, RAISIN' ALL KINDA HELL, TOTALLY OUTTA CONTROL.
SO, CASEY... HE STEPPED IN WHEN IT GOT REALLY BAD. KNOCKED SOME SENSE INTO ME BEFORE I GOT INTO SERIOUS TROUBLE. TURNED MY STUPID BUTT AROUND 'FORE IT WAS TOO LATE.
I MEAN, HE... HE LOST HIS MOM, TOO, YOU KNOW? HIS DAD WAS A TRAINWRECK AND, STILL, HE TOOK CARE OF ME WHEN I WAS ALL SCREWED UP. HE... HE SAVED ME.
WOW.
LADIES... YOU CAN SEE YOUR FRIEND NOW.

HOW IS HE, DOCTOR?
IT'S STILL TOO EARLY TO TELL. HE LOST A LOT OF BLOOD, BUT THE TRANSFUSIONS SHOULD TAKE CARE OF THAT.
THE STAB WOUNDS MAY BE ANOTHER STORY. NO VITAL ORGANS WERE DAMAGED, BUT HE DID SUFFER SIGNIFICANT TRAUMA, PARTICULARLY TO THE ABDOMINAL REGION.
HE ALSO SHOWED SIGNS OF BLUNT FORCE INJURIES TO THE HEAD. ARE YOU SURE HE WAS ONLY STABBED?
HE PLAYS HOCKEY.
NOT ANYMORE—WHETHER HE'S FORTUNATE ENOUGH TO SURVIVE THIS OR NOT.
I'LL LEAVE YOU ALONE NOW.
UM... PARDON ME.
POOR CASEY. DO YOU THINK WE SHOULD CALL HIS DAD, ANGEL?
I ALREADY CALLED MY POP AT THE BAR—TOLD HIM TO PASS THE MESSAGE TO CASEY'S DAD, BUT THAT WORTHLESS DRUNK'LL PROBABLY BE TOO WASTED TO GIVE A CRAP, ANYWAYS.
YOU KNOW, IT AIN'T RIGHT, APRIL. A GOOD GUY LIKE CASEY DON'T DESERVE TO SUFFER LIKE THIS...
...BUT THAT LOSER DAD OF HIS SURE AS HELL DOES.
"YES, FLEE..."

"...BUT YOU CANNOT ESCAPE THE TRUTH.

"LIKE A MONSTER SEEKING PREY IN THE NIGHT, THE TRUTH...
RRAARGH!
"...WILL HUNT YOU DOWN."

BUT... FAMILY IS EVERYTHING! I HAVE TO KILL HIM!

NO, FOOLISH BOY—YOU DO NOT KILL. EVER.

...THEN I WILL.

WHERE...?
HE IS GONE, LEONARDO...

I WON'T LET YOU HURT MY FAMILY!
I'LL KILL YOU AND THEM!
WHAT DO YOU THINK YOU ARE DOING, LEONARDO?!
SHEATHE YOUR WEAPON!
NO... YOU'RE WRONG!
IF YOU CAN'T PROTECT US...
...BUT YOU USED ALL NECESSARY MEANS TO DEFEND YOURSELF.
THIS IS NEVER WRONG.
TAKE THIS— A REMINDER OF WHAT YOU HAVE LEARNED TODAY.
STRENGTH IS EVERYTHING...

"...AND IT SHOULD ALWAYS BE USED TO PROTECT YOURSELF AND YOUR CLAN, NO MATTER THE COST."
HELP, LEO! PLEASE!
HE'S GONNA KILL US!
NOBODY.
HOLY... DID YOU GUYS SEE THAT?
BYE, LEO.
FZZZAK
NOOOOOO

NOBODY MESSES WITH MY BROTHERS!
NOBODY!
DO YOU HEAR ME?!
SWIIIP
SHHKK
HA HA HA HA HA HA HA HA HA HA HA HA HA HA HA HA
!
YOU! HOW—HOW *COULD* YOU?
HOW COULD YOU?
BECAUSE, THAT IS HIS NATURE, LEONARDO...
...TO FAIL YOU AT EACH AND EVERY TURN.
I... I DID WHAT I HAD TO DO—KILLED TO PROTECT MY CLAN, BUT... BUT I FAILED, TOO. THEY STILL DIED.
NO, YOU ACTED AS A TRUE AND LOYAL WARRIOR, LEONARDO. AND BECAUSE YOU DID, YOUR *TRUE* CLAN IS *NOT* DEAD.
"THE TIME HAS COME AT LAST TO OPEN YOUR EYES..."
FOOM

"...TO THE *TRUTH*."

I STILL THINK THIS IS A WASTE OF TIME. THAT FREAKIN' CAT'S NOTHIN' BUT TROUBLE—WHY THE HELL WOULD HE EVER WANNA HELP US?

I DO NOT KNOW, RAPHAEL, BUT I BELIEVE WE WILL SOON LEARN THE ANSWER—

—OLD HOB IS THERE... JUST AHEAD. MOVE WITH CAUTION, MY SONS.

I THINK WE LEFT CAUTION BEHIND AT THE CHURCH.

YO, HOB! YOU GOT TWO MINUTES BEFORE MY BETTER JUDGMENT KICKS IN!
HMPH. DIDN'T THINK YOU'D SHOW.
OH, CRAP! IS THAT–?

SLASH!
I *KNEW* LEO DIDN'T KILL HIM!
AND NOW WE KNOW HOW HOB FOUND THE CHURCH.

YOU CAN LOWER THAT HARDWARE—WE AIN'T HERE LOOKIN' FOR A SCRAP.
THEN WHAT *IS* IT THAT YOU SEEK, OLD HOB?
I'M LOOKIN' TO HELP YOU GET BACK THAT LOST PUP OF YOURS.
A LITTLE BIRD TOLD ME WHERE HE IS.
DAMN FLEABAG'S JUST FEEDIN' US A BUNCHA BULL. HE DON'T KNOW NOTHIN'.
YOU'RE WRONG.

LOOK, IT AIN'T NO SECRET WE'VE HAD OUR SHARE OF SQUABBLES. BUT THAT WAS THEN... AND THIS IS NOW.
IN CASE YOU HAVEN'T NOTICED, THINGS'RE GETTIN' PRETTY DAMN DICEY IN THE CITY—BIG OL' STREET WAR GETTIN' READY TO BLOW UP IN EVERYONE'S FACES. THE TIME TO PICK SIDES IS COMIN' REAL FAST, WHETHER YOU LIKE IT OR NOT.

SEE, WE'RE ALL MIXED UP IN SOMEONE ELSE'S FIGHT—THE STINKIN' HUMANS—BEIN' USED AND ABUSED LIKE THEIR LITTLE PETS TO GET THEM WHAT *THEY* WANT.
WELL... NO MORE.
THE HUMANS MIGHT NEED US, BUT WE SURE AS HELL DON'T NEED THEM. WE'RE STRONGER, SMARTER... ***BETTER*** IN EVERY WAY. A MUTANT ARMY WOULD SMASH THEM IN A HEARTBEAT.
THAT'S WHY I ASKED YOU HERE—I WANT YOU IN MY ARMY. NOT UNDER ME, BUT *WITH* ME. AND, TO PROVE I'M LEGIT, I'LL SHOW YOU WHERE LEONARDO IS. YOU'LL SEE REAL QUICK IT AIN'T ME AND SLASH YOU GOTTA WORRY ABOUT.

IT'S HUMANS...
...ALWAYS HUMANS.
YEP, I *KNEW* IT—NOTHIN' BUT BULL.

YET, IT APPEARS WE HAVE NO CHOICE BUT TO TRUST YOU, OLD HOB... FOR NOW.
TAKE ME TO MY SON—AND IF IT TURNS OUT YOU ARE NOT LYING AND WE ARE ABLE TO RETRIEVE HIM, THEN, PERHAPS, I WILL CONSIDER YOUR OFFER.
HEY...

...THAT'S ALL I'M ASKIN'.

WHERE...?
AH, I SEE YOU'VE RETURNED ALONE...
...AN UTTER FAILURE.
NO, YOU'RE WRONG. YOU'RE THE FAILURE.
ALL THIS TIME, ALL YOUR PROMISES TO PROTECT, TO TRAIN... ALL LIES. YOU PRETENDED TO BE MY MASTER... MY FATHER!
AND LIKE A TRUSTING IMBECILE, YOU BELIEVED IT ALL.
WHY LIE TO YOUR OWN SON? WHY?
FOOL— YOU ARE NOT MY SON. MY SONS...
...ARE DEAD.
NO.
SHLIP
THAX
CRASH
GRRARG!
AAAHHHG!
I'VE HAD ENOUGH!
ENOUGH!

HAHAHAHA!
A FAILURE! ALWAYS A FAILURE!
NO, HAMATO YOSHI...
GLRGK!
SHIK
ENOUGH.
...IT IS YOU WHO HAVE FAILED.
DO YOU SEE THE REALITY NOW, LEONARDO—THE TRUE MONSTER BEHIND THE LIES? THE PATHETIC VERMIN WHO WOULD HAVE YOU PERISH THROUGH WEAKNESS AND UNCERTAINTY?
YES.
THEN YOU ARE READY AT LAST.
YES...

...MASTER!

CHAPTER 4
<GRANDDAUGHTER.>

<GRANDFATHER, I... I DID NOT KNOW YOU WERE WATCHING ME.>

<YOUR TECHNIQUE— KOREAN, YES? GEOMMU?>
<YES, GRANDFATHER. IT IS ONE OF MANY FORMS I USE WHEN TRAINING.>

<I SEE.>

<TRAINING HAS ENDED FOR TODAY. THE TIME HAS COME TO USE YOUR KATANA FOR SOMETHING MORE IMPORTANT THAN DANCING ABOUT.>
<ARE YOU PREPARED FOR THE COMING BATTLE WITH YOSHI AND HIS BROOD?>

<OF COURSE I AM READY, MASTER SHREDDER.>
<IF I MAY ASK, HOW CAN YOU BE CERTAIN THE MUTANTS WILL FIND US?>

CITY FALL
PART THREE

I KNEW I'D FIND YOU HERE, CASEY.
YOU ALWAYS DID HIT THE RINK WHEN THINGS GOT ROUGH.
MOM?
SPAK
THAT SLAP SHOT OF YOURS IS GETTING PRETTY WICKED, KIDDO.
YOU'RE DEFINITELY YOUR FATHER'S SON WHEN IT COMES TO MUSCLES.
MOM... ABOUT DAD. I... I REALLY TRIED TO DO WHAT YOU ASKED, WHAT I PROMISED, BUT HE—
SHHH... YOUR DAD'S NO LONGER YOUR CONCERN, CASEY.
YOU DID EVERYTHING YOU COULD TO HELP HIM AND I'M SO PROUD OF YOU. BUT HE'S ON HIS OWN PATH NOW. HE'S NOT YOUR RESPONSIBILITY ANYMORE.
AND IT'S TIME FOR YOU TO WAKE UP, HON.
MOM, ARE... ARE YOU AN ANGEL NOW?
...ANGEL... NOW...
...ANGEL... THINK HE'S... WAKING UP NOW...
WH-WHERE... ?

OH, CASEY, THANK GOD!

GAHH... I FEEL LIKE CRUD. WHAT... WHAT HAPPENED?
YOU ALMOST DIED, THAT'S WHAT HAPPENED!
YEAH, JONES-- NEXT TIME YOU NEED ATTENTION, DO US ALL A FAVOR AND WRITE A POEM OR SOMETHIN', OKAY?

VERY... FUNNY, ANGEL. YOU SHOULD KNOW GETTIN' THE CRAP KICKED OUTTA YOU IS... WAY EASIER THAN WRITIN' STUFF.

OH, MAN! RAPH! WE... WE GOT JUMPED BY THE FOOT AND--
RAPH'S OKAY, CASEY--HE AND SPLINTER CAME WITH US WHEN WE BROUGHT YOU TO THE HOSPITAL. BUT THEY HAD TO GO LOOK FOR LEO.
LEO? WHY?

HE DISAPPEARED AFTER THEIR BIG FIGHT WITH SHREDDER AND KARAI.
DISAPPEARED? WHAT ARE Y--GAH!

CASEY, YOU JUST HAD MAJOR SURGERY--YOU NEED TO REST.
YEAH, MAN, YOU GOT HURT PRETTY BAD. WE GOT A TON TO CATCH YOU UP ON, SO JUST CHILL AND WE'LL TELL YA EVERYTHING.
YEAH... YEAH, OKAY. BUT... DO ME A FAVOR...

"...START WITH WHAT THE HECK'S GOIN' ON WITH THE TURTLES."
YOU SURE THIS IS THE RIGHT PLACE, HOB?
POSITIVE. WHAT MAKES YOU THINK I'M LYIN'?

WELL, I AIN'T.

FINE...
NOW WE JUST HAVE TO FIGURE OUT...

...HOW TO GET IN THERE.
TORTUGA
LEAVE THAT TO ME.
MAN, I SINCERELY DO NOT TRUST THIS FLEA-BITER.
YEAH—HE SURE SEEMS TO CONVENIENTLY HAVE ALL THE ANSWERS, DOESN'T HE?
I AGREE WITH YOUR CONCERNS, MY SONS. BUT I DO BELIEVE OLD HOB KNOWS WHERE LEONARDO IS—THAT IS ENOUGH TO CONVINCE ME TO FOLLOW HIM.
HEY... WHERE'S MIKEY?

RRRGGHHH...

DUDE, CHILLAX... YOU DON'T GOTTA BE SO GRUMPY. HAVE A CANDY BAR—YOU'LL LOVE IT.

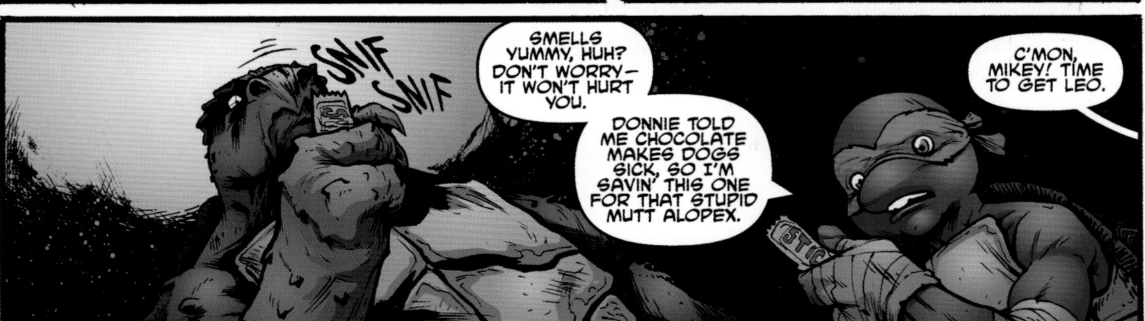
SNIF SNIF
SMELLS YUMMY, HUH? DON'T WORRY—IT WON'T HURT YOU.
DONNIE TOLD ME CHOCOLATE MAKES DOGS SICK, SO I'M SAVIN' THIS ONE FOR THAT STUPID MUTT ALOPEX.
C'MON, MIKEY! TIME TO GET LEO.

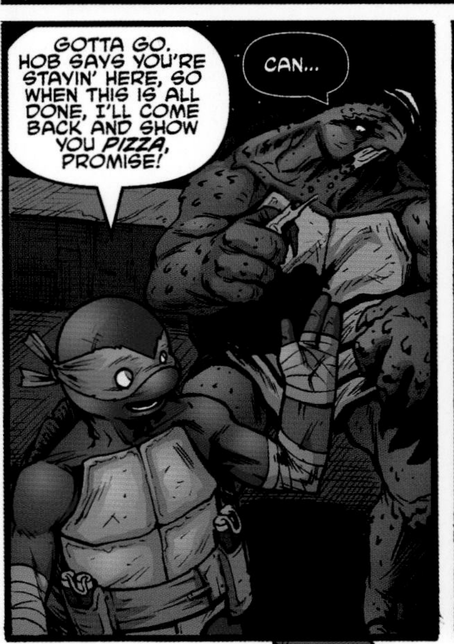
GOTTA GO. HOB SAYS YOU'RE STAYIN' HERE, SO WHEN THIS IS ALL DONE, I'LL COME BACK AND SHOW YOU PIZZA, PROMISE!
CAN...

...DEE!

HEY, GUYS, TURNS OUT SLASH AIN'T SUCH A BAD DUDE AFTER ALL. HE DIDN'T TRY TO EAT ME OR NOTHIN'.
ONLY YOU, MIKEY... ONLY YOU.
YO, LADIES...

...WE DOIN' THIS THING OR WHAT?
YES, OLD HOB. LEAD THE WAY...

"...WE WILL FOLLOW."

BREAKING AND ENTERING? SERIOUSLY?

YEAH, BECAUSE KNOCKING WOULD BE SO MUCH BETTER, RIGHT, TURTLE?

KLCK

AFTER YOU.

WHAT? NO MORE LEADIN' THE WAY?
HEY, IT'S A DARK ROOM AND YOU GOT THE POINTY KNIVES AND STICKS— I'LL GLADLY FOLLOW.

WHOA... IT *IS* DARK IN HERE.
MIKEY, QUIET!

WHAT THE—?!
SLAM
HOB!

DAMMIT, HOB! I *KNEW* YOU WERE FULL OF CRAP!
YOU SAY *CRAP*, LITTLE TURTLE, I SAY *BRAINS*. YOU MIGHT BE A BUNCHA DEATH-WISH IDIOTS...
SNP
...BUT I SURE AS HELL AIN'T NO DUMMY.

STINKIN' FLEABAG, I OUGHTA–
LET HIM GO, RAPHAEL. OLD HOB DID WHAT HE PROMISED.

HAMATO YOSHI... SO KIND OF YOU TO JOIN US.
UH-OH.

IT IS NOT KINDNESS THAT DRIVES THIS VISIT, OROKU SAKI.
SHOW YOURSELF—I WOULD SPEAK WITH YOU NOW.
BUT OF COURSE.
KLIK
WELCOME, YOSHI, TO THE BEGINNING...
...AND THE END.

I DON'T SEE LEO ANYWHERE.
NAH... JUST PINHEAD, HIS BOWL-CUT BRAT, AND THAT MANGY POOCH.
REMAIN CALM AND ON GUARD. I WILL SPEAK TO SAKI--DO NOT INSTIGATE ANYTHING YET, MY SONS.
IS THAT UNDERSTOOD, RAPHAEL?
BUT I, UH... UM...
...YEAH, OKAY. UNDERSTOOD.

WE ARE HERE FOR MY SON, OROKU SAKI... FOR LEONARDO. WE HAVE BEEN TOLD YOU HOLD HIM PRISONER. WE DEMAND HIS IMMEDIATE RETURN.
BLOOD NEED NOT BE SHED THIS DAY, BUT BE AWARE--WE WILL USE ALL MEANS NECESSARY TO RETRIEVE OUR LOVED ONE.

AH, BUT I WOULD EXPECT NO LESS, YOSHI, THOUGH I MUST INFORM YOU THAT BLOOD HAS *ALREADY* BEEN SPILLED.

I TOLD YOU TONIGHT BELONGS TO BEGINNINGS AND ENDINGS, DID I NOT?

"EVEN AS WE SPEAK, MY NINJA ARE MOVING TO TIGHTEN MY GRIP ALL ACROSS THIS GREAT CITY...

"...CUTTING DOWN ANY AND ALL WHO DARE OPPOSE MY RULE.

"MY LONG-AWAITED DESTINY IS FINALLY AT HAND...

"...AND I WILL CRUSH ANYONE FOOLISH ENOUGH TO STAND IN MY WAY."

SADLY, HOWEVER, YOU WILL NOT BE ALIVE TO WITNESS MY ULTIMATE TRIUMPH, YOSHI.
TONIGHT I END THE NUISANCE YOU HAVE PRESENTED TO ME OVER TWO LIFETIMES.
YOU ARE SORELY MISTAKEN IF YOU BELIEVE FOR EVEN ONE SECOND THAT I CARE FOR YOUR CRIMINAL WARS OR YOUR ARROGANT THREATS.
RETURN MY SON TO ME, OROKU SAKI.

YOUR SON IS *NO MORE*, YOSHI.

THIS... THIS CANNOT BE.

HEAR ME NOW, DEVIL. IF I CANNOT HAVE MY SON...
...I WILL HAVE YOUR HEAD!
NO...

...I WILL NOT ALLOW YOU TO HARM MY MASTER.

MY SON... YOU LIVE.
BUT WHY ARE YOU—
GRFF!
NO, RODENT...
...YOU ARE WRONG.
SHRHIIPP
I AM NOT YOUR SON.

OH, HELL NO!
IT'S STILL LEO, GUYS!
DON'T HURT HIM, RAPH!
WHAT THE HELL, LEO?! THAT'S OUR FATHER!
I ALREADY SAID...
...HE IS NOT MY FATHER!
THWACK
WHAT'S GOING ON?!
MIKEY...
...WATCH OUT!
SWIIIP

LEO! STOP THIS!
FWAP
GRK
GRRKK...
NO!
SHING
WHOMP
THUD

ALL RIGHT, BIG BRO, YOU WANT ROUGH...
...I'LL GIVE YOU ROUGH!
SCHINK
WHA-?!
CHING
GUH!
CRUCH
FWUMP

LEO, PLEASE... NO...

ENOUGH!
LOWER YOUR SWORD, LEONARDO. YOU HAVE PROVEN YOURSELF A WORTHY CHUNIN.

MASTER— WHY DO YOU NOT ALLOW LEONARDO TO EXECUTE HIM?
BECAUSE, KARAI...

"...THE RAT IS MINE."
YOU MAY HAVE THE REST.

KLIK
DAMN.
GUYS...
...RUN!

WHERE?!
THE DOOR WE CAME IN! WE'LL BUST IT OPEN— C'MON!
RAGH!

NO!
OH, MAN, THEY'RE EVERYWHERE!
JUST MEANS PLENTY OF BUTT TO KICK! BRING IT!
YES, MUTANT...

RAAARGH!
SLASH!
CAN-DEE?!
YOU KNOW IT, BIG DUDE! SOON AS WE GET OUTTA HERE!
THE WALL'S GIVING WAY! NOW OR NEVER, GUYS!
LET'S GO, SLASH!
THIS *AIN'T OVER*, PUNKS!

OKAY, WE'RE IN THE CLEAR.
HOB! I'M GONNA SKIN YOU ALIVE!
WHOA! EASY! WHY YOU SO TICKED OFF AT ME? YOU'RE STILL BREATHIN', AIN'TCHA?

YOU TOOK US TO A FREAKIN' MEAT GRINDER!
AND I GOT YOU OUTTA THE MEAT GRINDER!

I TOLD THE FOOT I COULD DELIVER YOU, AND I DID. THAT GETS THE TOP DOG OFF THIS CAT'S BACK. WITH WHAT'S COMIN' TO THIS CITY, THAT'S PRICELESS. NOT MY FAULT HE DIDN'T KNOW I HAD ANOTHER TURTLE UP MY SLEEVE.
WAY I SEE IT, I'M SQUARE WITH EVERYONE. AND THE OFFER TO YOU TO JOIN MY GANG STILL STANDS.

YOU CAN TAKE YOUR OFFER AND SHOVE IT, FLEABAG. WE'LL NEVER JOIN YOUR FREAKSHOW.
AND QUIT FLATTERING YOURSELF, HOB— THAT WAS SLASH SAVING OUR BUTTS BACK THERE, NOT YOU.
HERE YOU GO, BUDDY. GOOD BOY.
CAN... DEE!

NO LUCK GETTIN' THE OTHER LITTLE GREENIE BACK, HUH? LET ME GUESS—HE WENT AND GOT HIMSELF A NEW DADDY, RIGHT?
DAMMIT, HOB, NOT NOW, ALL RIGHT?
JUST...
...NOT NOW.
TO BE CONTINUED!

ART BY KEVIN EASTMAN · COLORS BY RONDA PATTISON

THIS PAGE AND OPPOSITE PAGE: ART BY **KEVIN EASTMAN**

ART BY KEVIN EASTMAN

OPPOSITE PAGE: ART BY ANDY KUHN • COLORS BY DANIEL "PEZ" LOPEZ

ART BY DEAN HASPIEL • COLORS BY ALLEN PASSALAQUA

OPPOSITE PAGE: ART BY KEVIN EASTMAN • COLORS BY RONDA PATTISON

D.W.P.

ART BY KEVIN EASTMAN · COLORS BY RONDA PATTISON

OPPOSITE PAGE: ART BY RICH WOODALL

LAWNZ
AFTER McFARLANE

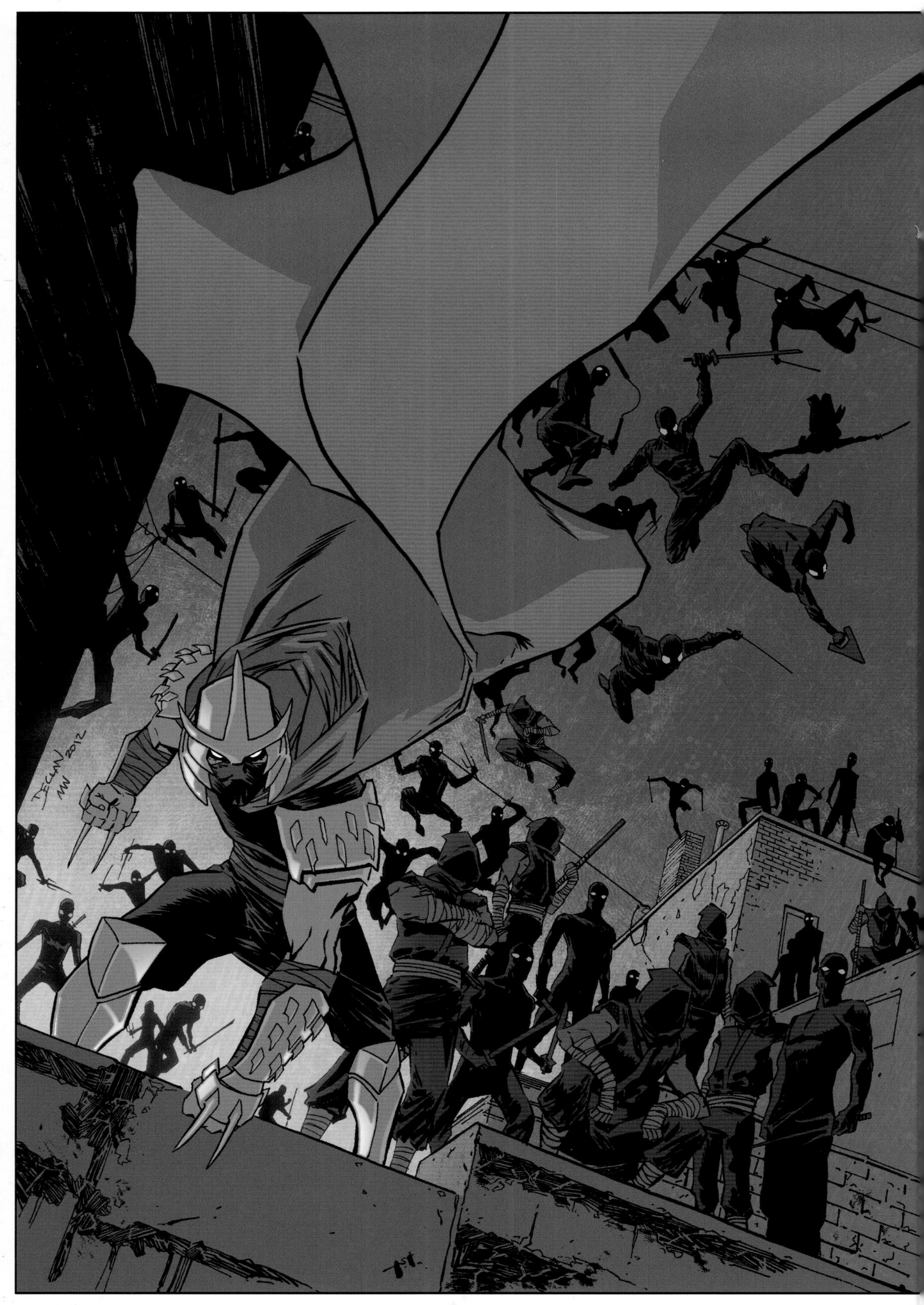

ART BY DECLAN SHALVEY · COLORS BY NOLAN WOODWARD

OPPOSITE PAGE: ART BY KEVIN EASTMAN · COLORS BY RONDA PATTISON

THIS PAGE AND OPPOSITE PAGE: ART BY MATEUS SANTOLOUCO

CITY
FALL

ART BY DAVE WACHTER

OPPOSITE PAGE: ART BY KEVIN EASTMAN · COLORS BY RONDA PATTISON

ART BY FREDDIE WILLIAMS II